Building Community Resilience through Social Media

Table of Contents

There's a social revolution going on right now. Can you use your resources, your contacts, your rights to spread knowledge - to help others who can help others? I think the next decade is going to be run by nerds and geeks, who today are building community resilience and influencing global change through social media.

— Jack Dorsey

Chapter 1. Introduction

Welcome to this Special Report, a must-read compendium lighting your path to a fascinating journey - "Building Community Resilience through Social Media". This material doesn't just skim the surface but dives deep, unraveling the incredible potential of social media as a tool for carving resilient communities, ultimately shaping a stronger society. Discover how ordinary exchanges of tweets, posts, and likes can be harnessed to mobilize collective action, spread crucial information, and inspire change. With real-life cases and practical guidance, it's about transforming your social media scrolling into purposeful engagement. Help fortify your community, and through it, the world—one like, share or follow at a time. Intrigued? Then this Special Report is just for you!

Chapter 2. The Rising Influence of Social Media in Community Building

As we set sail on the vast, endless ocean of social media, it is crucial to initially elucidate its expansive significance in modern society, thus pulling into clarity why it is an invaluable tool in community-building endeavors. Today, social media is no longer just a virtual venue for casual, inconsequential chatter; instead, it has transformed into a vibrant, bustling marketplace of ideas — a virtual agora teeming with human connection, patronage of unique causes, and social capital that fosters solidarity.

2.1. The Evolution of Social Media

From the onset, social media embraced a humble beginning. The launch of platforms such as MySpace in the early 21st century marked the dawn of a new era where individuals were provided spheres to express themselves digitally. As we progressed towards a more connected age, the advent and proliferation of platforms including Facebook, Twitter, and Instagram, further revolutionized the way we communicate and interact. Social media broke through the confinements of space and time, allowing messages to fly at lightning speed, thereby creating a world that is more intricately linked than ever before. Today, social media isn't just a facet of our lives — it is knitted into the very fabric of our social existence.

2.2. Socialization through Social Media

People are social creatures by nature. The insatiable desire for fellowship and connection led to the formation of societal networks, which have now expanded beyond physical confines via social media. More than just a digital extension of interpersonal interaction, it serves as an incubator for diverse communities. From hobbyist groups, professional networks, advocacy forums to locality-based groups - social media facilitates a broad spectrum of communities. Through a myriad of posts, shares, tweets, and comments, individuals around the globe not only share information but also experiences, perspectives, and emotions. This dynamic engagement instigates a sense of belongingness and social cohesion.

2.3. Social Capital: The Building Block of Communities

The theory of social capital posits that relationships hold value and connections foster mutual benefits. In the digital landscape, social capital manifests as the collective value of all interactions within a social network. These interactions encompass sharing beneficial information, endorsing or promoting others' ideas or content, offering assistance or advice, and establishing relational trust. The accrual of social capital within a community paves the way towards fostering resilience, as it bolsters interdependence, facilitates exchange of resources, and cultivates shared trust and norms — all ingredients vital for robust community resilience.

2.4. The Power of Social Media in Mobilizing Collective Action

What makes social media truly exceptional is its potential to incite collective action. The Arab Spring, #MeToo movement, and various climate strikes undeniably showcase social media's power as an accelerator for social change. As an accessible, far-reaching medium, it provides individuals with the tools to campaign for shared causes, organize movements, or rally support for community efforts. Social media enables the dissemination of information and mobilization at an unprecedented scale, fostering a communal voice that echoes across borders.

2.5. Embracing Social Media as a Pillar of Community Building

Conclusively, the ascent of social media as a cornerstone for community building is not surprising. It provides a platform for meaningful social interaction, enriches the social capital of communities, and acts as a catalyst for collective action. It is evident that amidst the ebb and flow of digital trends, social media continues to reshape how communities are formed, how they interact, and how they mature. As we move forward into an increasingly digitized future, harnessing the power of social media could be our key to fostering more resilient communities.

As we journey into the core of this comprehensive material, bear in mind the understanding that we've now built around the rising influence of social media in community building. This understanding will be integral as we delve further into how we can strategically and responsibly utilize this influential medium in fostering resilient communities.

Chapter 3. Understanding Community Resilience: A Primer

Community resilience is an intricate concept with many facets, each unfolding in its own unique way, pivoting on the circumstances at play. Consider community resilience as the capacity of a community to anticipate, withstand, respond to, and recover from adversities, disturbances, or disruptions while retaining or returning to a desired state of equilibrium. By focusing on a wide spectrum of conditions, including everything from natural calamities and pandemics to economic downturns and social unrest, the integral elements of community resilience emerge.

3.1. The Fundamentals of Community Resilience

To look at the fundamentals of community resilience, let's begin by looking at what a community is. In essence, a community can be any grouping of individuals that share spatial, social, or virtual connections. Salient examples would include a group of neighbors sharing the same geographical location, an association of business owners in a market, or even netizens participating in a Twitter thread about climate change.

Next, let's dissect the notion of resilience. Resilience can be visualized as a rubber band's ability to return to its original shape after being stretched. This transformative potential enables communities to withstand the shock of disruption and regain their original state, or even evolve and adapt to a new equilibrium that might be better suited to the new realities.

Understanding these elements, community resilience can then be conceptualized as a multi-dimensional phenomenon involving an array of internal and external factors working together to bolster the community's overall capacity to recover from adversity. This involves not just physical resources but also the social, economic, and cultural resources available to the community members.

3.2. The Pillars of Community Resilience

Community resilience is underpinned by several vital pillars:

1. **Social Cohesion:** A community's collective identity and the bonds that tie its members together are the cornerstone of social cohesion. This interconnectedness creates a shared responsibility towards each other, fostering collective action in times of crisis.

2. **Information and Communication:** An essential pillar of community resilience, information, and communication technology could facilitate effective disaster risk reduction strategies, offer platforms for information sharing, and assist in coordinated response to threats.

3. **Economic Development:** A community's economic stability affects its capacity to come through adversity. Inclusive and sustainable community development that offers opportunities for earning and financial safety nets is critical in fostering resilience.

4. **Competent Leadership:** The ability of local leaders to inspire trust, mobilize resources, and guide a coordinated response effort is crucial. A leader's role in facilitating the development of resilience strategies cannot be overstated.

5. **Community Infrastructure:** Physical factors like functional transportation, robust telecommunications network, and effective public utilities systems are all crucial. Also, community services and facilities that provide social support, such as schools,

hospitals, and local centers, contribute to community resilience.

3.3. The Journey from Vulnerability to Resilience

The journey from vulnerability to resilience is about the capacity of individuals and communities to navigate their way towards resources that promote their wellbeing. It isn't just about how hard a disruption hits a community, but how well the community can absorb, recover, and adapt from the disruption.

While disruptions may momentarily incapacitate communities, they can also serve as catalysts for change, pushing communities to find innovative solutions, engage in corrective actions, and collaborate on a broader scale. It is through such collective responses that communities can harness the power of resilience to transcend their vulnerabilities and evolve stronger than before.

3.4. Leveraging Social Capital for Community Resilience

The resilience of a community is deeply embedded in the social capital it has cultivated over time. Social capital refers to the network of relationships and the associated norms of trust and reciprocity that exist within a community. It is both an outcome of and a catalyst for community resilience.

Building social capital requires fostering trust, promoting reciprocal aid, encouraging civic participation, and creating a sense of belonging among community members. It is through social capital that communities can mobilize resources, share information, and collectively respond in times of crisis. Moreover, social capital facilitates learning and adaptation, which are key elements of resilience.

In conclusion, understanding community resilience is pivotal to help communities prepare for, respond to, and recover from adversities. Highlighting the critical role of social cohesion, communication, economic stability, leadership, infrastructure, and social capital, it lays out the blueprint for fostering resilience within communities. Such resilience not only equips communities to face disruptions but also transforms adversities into opportunities for growth and expansion. Through promoting resilience, we are ultimately fostering a more inclusive, stronger, and better-adapted society, one community at a time.

Chapter 4. Reinforcing Connections: The Social Fabric of Resilient Communities

To successfully build a robust community, one must first understand the social fabric that binds it together. This chapter aims to provide a comprehensive exposition on the interconnected web of relationships and shared experiences that compose a community, highlighting how these elements can be reinforced through social media to ameliorate community resilience.

4.1. The Essence of Social Connection

The social connection refers to the cohesive bond that exists within a community, built on the foundation of personal relationships, common interests, shared values, and trust. It's the magnet that holds individuals together, transforming a disparate group of people into a united front capable of navigated shared challenges. The strength and integrity of these social connections often serve as a reliable measure of a community's resilience.

Each individual within the community is akin to a thread in a fabric—the more threads, the denser the material and the stronger it becomes. These threads are intricately woven together through daily interactions, communal activities, shared histories, and collective experiences that create a dynamic and fluid tapestry. This is the social fabric of the community—adaptable, resilient, and capable of withstanding wear and tear.

4.2. Social Fabric and Community Resilience

Community resilience is, in essence, the ability of a community to spring back from setbacks or dance with disturbances in ways that foster learning, adaptation, and improvement. Strengthening the social fabric is critical to buoy this resilience. The stronger the social fabric, the higher the community's capacity to absorb external shocks and bounce back quickly.

The intertwining threads of social networks provide an essential safety net for individuals in times of crisis. These networks prove to be lifelines—offering advice, resources, understanding, and comfort when needed the most. Active engagement within these networks maintains ties, fosters unity, and sparks action towards collective goals; it consequently reinforces the community resilience.

4.3. Social Media: A Platform to Reinforce Social Connections

Social media emerges as an unprecedented tool in shaping the social fabric and bolstering resilience. It offers a multitude of features that stimulate connection, promote dialogue, enable collaboration, and diffuse information quickly and broadly—an encapsulation of the intrinsic elements in nurturing a resilient community.

Social media platforms can facilitate potent connections by extending the reach of interpersonal relationships beyond geographical boundaries. They provide venues where people from diverse backgrounds, but with similar interests, values, or issues can converge, creating an amalgamation of voices that can amplify shared causes or crowdsource solutions.

The concept of "bonding" and "bridging" social capital is highly applicable here. Bonding social capital refers to the relationship within homogenous groups—those who share the same identity, culture, or experience. Bridging social capital, conversely, relates to the connections among diverse groups, fostering an understanding and respect of diversity within and between communities. Both can be facilitated and amplified via social media, enhancing the grid of connection points that solidify the social fabric.

An interesting feature of social media activity is that it leaves digital footprints that can map out social networks and their dynamics. Through analysis of these digital traces, community leaders, public health officials, and researchers can gain insights into the community's social fabric, enabling more strategic and responsive action.

4.4. Amplifying the Effect: Tips and Techniques

To harness social media's potential in reinforcing the social fabric, it's important to adopt the right strategies. For instance, building a network with a diverse array of voices promotes various perspectives and experiences, stirring richer discussions and more comprehensive solutions. Encouraging active engagement through reciprocal communication, likes, comments, sharing, and other meaningful virtual interactions boosts the visibility and resonance of various ideas or concerns. Sharing authentic stories and experiences creates bonding experiences and fosters a sense of belonging. Using hashtags effectively allows individuals to follow or contribute to topics, causes, or discussions relevant to them.

On a larger scale, initiatives could be developed to design campaigns promoting shared community values or simulating inclusive discussions about community challenges. Such endeavors could increase community awareness, mobilize collective action, or spark changes in policies and practices.

4.5. Conclusion

As we navigate the digital age, the potential offered by social media in shaping our social tapestry is clear. By understanding its dynamic capabilities and learning how to utilize them efficiently, we can reinforce social connections and foster community resilience. Our journey continues in the chapter about the role of social media in crisis management, throwing light on how social media can serve as an emergency tool in times of disaster. Yet for now, let's pause and appreciate how every like, follow, share, or even simple online greeting can reinforce our social fabric—one social media post at a time.

Chapter 5. The Role of Social Media in Crisis Management and Response

Perhaps now, more than any other time in our shared history, a compelling examination of the critical role of social media in crisis management and response is paramount. The following discourse not only guides you through the wide alleyways of its concept but illuminates the hidden crannies where its true power of community strengthening can be harnessed.

5.1. The Crisis Management and Social Media Dynamic

It would be inappropriate, if not anachronistic, to talk about crisis management today without giving meaningful attention to the role played by gigantic waves of data flowing from social media platforms. Social media, acting as a digital agora, provides a vast, rapid, and virtually unfiltered platform where information can circulate freely. In the era of the smartphone, crises such as natural calamities, health pandemics, terrorist attacks, or disasters of institutional failures that could have remained purely local in impact two decades ago, now send shockwaves globally within minutes, thanks to social media.

But what is more profound is how social media emerges as a critical tool for crisis response and management. It is the spark that ignites grassroots-level mobilizations, the beacon that guides relief efforts, and the echo chamber that amplifies calls for assistance and solidarity. It allows for an instantaneous, wide-range sharing of information on crises, enabling authorities to take swift action, benefiting both the communities affected and those charged with managing the crisis.

5.2. Strategies in Harnessing Social Media for Crisis Response

Like any tool, the utility of social media in crisis situations depends on how well it is leveraged. A haphazard approach might lead to misinformation, panic, or misdirection of efforts. Hence, strategic and purpose-driven use becomes a necessity rather than an option.

The wisdom here lies in establishing clear information channels and leveraging the influence of social media figures and platforms. It means being proactive in designating reliable 'official' social media handles or pages for credible updates, and in cultivating partnerships with influencers who can spread vital information quickly and to a broad audience. Like any other aspect of crisis management, this requires prior planning, including social listening tools to monitor online chatter and sentiment, and training personnel to effectively communicate and engage online in times of crisis.

5.3. Crowd-Sourced Crisis Response and Social Media

In crisis circumstances, sheer geographic expanse or the numbers affected can overwhelm the most capable of authorities. Social media's unique power in transforming end-users into force multipliers comes to play here. By crowd-sourcing, an otherwise overwhelming operation reduces to manageable proportions. Images and live reports shared by individuals at the disaster scene can guide first responders, ensuring aid reaches where it is most needed. In the right circumstances, social media users can mount fundraising campaigns, field volunteers, and even reassure worried friends and relatives about the safety of their loved ones.

5.4. Navigating the Perils: Hoaxes, Trolls, and Misinformation

Brimming with potential as it is, the open and fast-paced universe of social media also poses challenges of hoaxes, trolls, and misinformation, which tend to thrive particularly in crisis situations when people are frantic for information. Crisis management teams ought to be prepared to swiftly and assertively debunk these, reassuring the public while maintaining the integrity of the response operations. Again, this underlines the importance of official information channels, robust online presence, and consistent messaging.

Having traversed this analysis, however, it's clear that, despite the perils, the power in the people's hands that social media represents is a net positive in crisis management and response, properly harnessed. Thus, the keyword is preparedness, both in the strategic use of social media tools and in combating the potential negatives they can bring. The more society understands and is able to navigate this technology, the stronger and more resilient we'll be in facing the inevitable crises that lie ahead.

Chapter 6. Thriving through Disruption: Social Media in Disaster Resilience

In this compendium of wisdom, we explore and unpack the important yet somewhat nebulous role of social media in bolstering community resilience, with a particular focus on how it can enable communities to thrive amidst the turbulent waves of crises and disasters.

6.1. The Face of Crisis Management in a Social Media World

The twenty-first century, synonymous with the digital era, has borne witness to a radical paradigm shift in crisis and disaster management. In contrast to the traditional reliance on long-established institutions such as government agencies or physical print media to route information related to disasters, the widespread adoption and endless capacities of social media have transformed this landscape.

Social media as a platform isn't just about sharing anecdotes or amusing animal videos, but has shown time and again its capacity to serve a more critical function. Its pervasive reach, real-time nature, accessibility and widespread adoption have led its transformation into an indispensable disaster communication tool.

Imagine this scenario: a seismic shudder crushes a small town, causing destabilizing aftershocks. Where once information would trundle bottom upwards, from the affected masses to the concerned authorities, social media's democratization of information flows has led to a sweeping role reversal. Today, those affected by a disaster can transmit information rapidly through their social media channels, an act that is equivalent to lighting distress flares into the digital sky.

During such catastrophes, social media provides real-time reporting of the situation on the ground, well ahead of traditional media. Pictures, videos, and textual descriptions uploaded by witnesses propagate swiftly across platforms. Such content equips intellectuals, volunteers, and relief organizations with a more accurate understanding of the prevailing ground reality, which in turn influences their disaster management strategies.

6.2. Building a Shield of Resilience through Social Media Collaboration

In reinforcing resilience, collaboration is a key element. A disaster might strike without notice, but the collective resilience of a community, strengthened by social media, stands as a firm shield against the unexpectedly devastating blow.

Social media enables proficient situational-awareness, galvanizing various actors around a common goal during a crisis. Emergency services, governmental bodies, non-governmental organizations, and the citizenry coalesce on these platforms, forming ad-hoc digital communities. These communities work collectively, sharing relevant information, pooling resources, even coordinating on-the-ground efforts, all aimed towards alleviating the situation.

The power of crowdsourcing is another incredible aspect of such platforms during crises. A plea for help, an announcement of missing persons, a call for provisions, even mapping the extent and impact of disaster—all can be crowdsourced via social media platforms. In doing so, collective intelligence and action are harnessed; the efforts are coordinated, targeted, and thus more effective.

The engagement with social media also extends to the aftermath of the disaster, a critical phase where the motto is 'restore and rebuild.' Through these platforms, continuous updates on recovery efforts can be disseminated, appeals for prolonged assistance can be made, and stories of hope, resilience, and gratitude can be shared. This not only maintains the momentum of the recovery process but also aids in psychological healing—a crucial aspect often overshadowed by immediate physical needs.

6.3. Fostering Preparedness and Adaptation: Social Media as a Proactive Tool

While social media is a formidable tool in responding to crises, its potential to foster disaster preparedness and adaptation, thereby enhancing overall resilience, should not be underestimated. It provides an accessible platform for disseminating crucial information on disaster preparedness and risk reduction, fostering a culture of proactive planning and awareness among communities.

Educational campaigns, tips, strategies, drills, and information regarding potential threats can be easily spread through these platforms, reaching a large audience with speed and efficacy. Thus, individuals and communities are better equipped and ready to adapt to unprecedented situations, heightening their capacity to not just recover from, but also proactively respond to crises.

6.4. Evolving a Framework: Maximizing the Potential of Social Media for Disaster Resilience

Despite its potential, the use of social media for disaster resilience is not without issues. Fake news, information overload, verification difficulties, digital divides, and privacy issues are among the challenges that need addressing. For social media to be effective in disaster situations, a comprehensive framework should be developed – one that takes into account these challenges, the various roles and players, ethical standards, and privacy norms.

Such a framework should provide guidelines on content vetting, verification processes, and establishment of trusted sources. It should outline ways to leverage algorithms for effective information sorting and dissemination during crises. It should also define roles and responsibilities, and put in place mechanisms to address misinformation and the digital divide.

With the right strategies in place, social media can transcend beyond its superficial appeal and become a transformative avenue for disaster resilience, promoting a culture of preparedness and collective solidarity, and ultimately helping communities not only survive but thrive through the trials of unexpected disruptions.

Indeed, in the rapidly evolving world of today, the amalgamation of resilient communities and social media advocacy is comparable to a symphony – a harmonious convergence of various elements leading to the formation of a compelling, cohesive whole. The robust notes of shared information, the steady rhythm of collaboration, the resounding crescendos of collective action – all compose a symphony of resilience that reverberates across the digital sphere, inspiring communities to rise, rebuild, and even thrive amidst the rubble of disruption.

Chapter 7. Promoting Positive Behavioral Change through Social Platforms

The turn of the century welcomed an era of connectivity that has redefined how we live our lives. Social platforms have transformed from merely being a mode of entertainment to becoming catalysts for positive behavioral change. In this era of constant flux and social transformations, fostering positive behavioral changes through social media has become highly pertinent.

7.1. Harnessing the Power of Social Media

Technologies and platforms, such as Facebook, Twitter, Instagram, LinkedIn, and others, have provided unprecedented opportunities for individuals and groups to connect, communicate, and collaborate. With billions of people worldwide with access to these platforms, it makes these social networks a canalization of sorts, carrying potent potential for mass behavioral change.

The viral nature of content on these platforms can contribute to shaping behavioral norms among networked individuals. It only takes one opprobrious joke or one insightful commentary to influence countless perspectives across the globe. Social media itinerates not just what we think, but also how we act, interconnect, and perceive our world.

7.2. Driving Behavioral Change through Social Platforms

Can the power of peer influence combined with strategic messaging on social media steer society through the rocky road ahead towards a more sustainable future? Can myriad inspirational posts, powerful images, and emotive videos work in shifting the behavioral landscape?

Let's delve into the heart of how social media can incite personal growth, positive societal change, and contribute to community resilience. We call this the process of 'social norming' - the phenomenon where group members adopt certain behaviors to align with the perceived norm of the group. As peer pressure influences the offline world, it similarly functions in online spaces, altering perceptions, attitudes, and actions. The caveat, however, is understanding the specifics of this online user influence to foster positive change effectively.

When it comes to behavioral change, credibility and emotional resonance are pivotal. Behavioral and social scientists affirm that emotional, cognitive, structural, and cultural factors contribute to this change. Social media can stimulate these factors through various content.

7.3. Case Study: #Trashtag Movement

To shed light on how this works in action, let's consider the '#Trashtag Challenge.' Here, individuals or groups pick a littered area, clean it up, and share 'before' and 'after' pictures on social media with the hashtag #Trashtag. The impact was swift and significant.

This movement tapped into the powerful mechanics of viral content – it was easy to understand, required affordable participation, encouraged communal activity, sparked an emotional response, and offered visible, shareable results. It targeted and triggered all the requisite factors for stirring behavioral change, painting a picture of a possible future – a cleaner world.

The #Trashtag movement soon spiraled into an international phenomenon, triggering individuals around the globe to partake in their local clean-ups. The hashtag witnessed an outpouring of millions of posts. Positive peer pressure in action, it demonstrated social norming on a grand scale, leading to both individual and community-scale changes in attitudes towards littering and conservation.

7.4. Devolving Strategies to Engage Audience

With information on the immense potential of social media platforms, the next piece of the puzzle lies in creating a strategic blueprint that effectively engages its audience.

When developing such strategies, it is integral to prioritize your audience. Understand their demographics, needs, values, and motivations. Ensure your content resonates with the intended audience and is relevant to their lives. Tools for audience analytics on most social media platforms can provide valuable insights.

Getting the messaging right is a crucible in which convincing content is forged. Essentially, it's about creating a compelling narrative that provokes emotion and spurs action. The message should be clear and concise, making sure to incorporate the 'why', 'what', and 'how' of the intended change.

Interaction is key to maintaining audience engagement. Encourage active audience participation through comments, shares, likes, retweets, or applying hashtags. Such interactivity not only fosters a sense of community but also enhances the content's reach.

Further, visualizations significantly amplify the impact of the message. Images, infographics, and videos are much more likely to be shared and remembered. They are more compelling regarding narrative storytelling, capable of unraveling intricate information simply.

Finally, consistency and persistence are crucial. Change rarely occurs overnight. Long-term commitment, regular posting, and perseverance are necessary to keep the momentum and to instigate real, lasting change.

7.5. The Challenge Ahead: Navigating the Roadblocks

While social media offers promising potential in inspiring positive behavioral change, understanding and navigating its inherent challenges are equally crucial. Firstly, social media platforms are replete with information, leading to an information overload. It's a contest for attention, and only the most compelling, relevant content breaks through the noise.

Secondly, the rapid demise of content is another obstacle. The ephemeral nature of social media means that most posts have a very short lifespan. This requires a consistent supply of fresh, captivating content to keep the audience's interest alive.

Moreover, it's worth acknowledging the prevalence of digital divide and misinformation. Digital divide refers to an uneven distribution in access to, use of, or impact of information and communication technologies. This, and the misinformation on social media, contribute to the challenges in mastering social platforms for behavioral change.

Despite these challenges, the potential benefits overshadow the drawbacks, highlighting the need for an adaptive strategy that is mindful of these obstacles, to effectively utilize social media platforms for positive behavioral change.

7.6. Looking Ahead: Reinforcing Positive Social Norms through Social Media

Social platforms are more than what they seem – they don't just reflect trends and normative behaviors; they have the power to create them. Our exploration underscores the real potential of wielding this democratized digital platform for encouraging positive behaviors in society.

Whether it is movements toward sustainable living, promoting wellness, yawning gaps in health education, or combating prejudices, social platforms have versatile potential. They can be the echo chambers of the best human traits, prompting a harmonious symphony of constructive thought and action. As we continually experiment and explore the relationship between social media and behavior change, we move closer to tapping into this full potential.

By continually refining our strategies, widening our understanding, and staying attuned to the changing social landscape, we are sure to unlock the complete potential of social media. It promises to provide us with a potent tool to foster community resilience and collective growth in a world increasingly tethered by digital threads.

Given the reach, immediacy, and ubiquity of these platforms, using social media for promoting positive behavioral change isn't just an opportunity—it is an imperative. Rightly employed, it will strengthen individual growth, stir social betterment, and cement the foundation of more resilient communities, one post at a time. With social media acting as our driver, we will be striding earnestly towards a more enterprising tomorrow, where the audacity of hope thrives, and positive change becomes a part of our universal social language.

Chapter 8. The Power of Social Media in Community Engagement and Activism

Social media has been an epoch-making revolution, providing a platform for people from all walks of life to express their views, find like-minded individuals, converse, engage, and rally for causes they cherish. As users, we might simply view these platforms as media for interactions, keeping in touch with friends and family, or sharing our daily lives. However, this chapter aims to aid you in appreciating the profundity of its impact, largely focused on how it empowers community engagement and activism.

8.1. The Dawning of Digital Activism

The inception of digital activism complexly altered the topography of civic engagement and social movements. No longer constrained by geographical boundaries or mass media gatekeeping, the average Internet user transcended into an agent for change. Pioneers in digital activism made the best of the convenience these platforms offered and their reach to catalyze movements that made their mark in the annals of history.

Arab Spring is a prime example of how social media's potency in activism was globally recognized. As a spontaneous series of protests primarily driven by youth in the Middle East, the Arab Spring relied heavily on social platforms like Twitter and Facebook to mobilize masses, organize protests, and voice dissent. It showed the world that individuals, armed only with a cause and valuable platforms (no pun intended), could steer societal change.

8.2. The Facets of Social Media Activism

Social media activism transpires in various forms, reflecting its adaptability to diverse causes and contexts. 'Hashtag Activism' epitomizes one of its most emblematic stances. Activists employ hashtags to consolidate discussions, spread awareness, and encourage participation around a particular cause. It has been instrumental in amplifying some of the vital movements of the past decade, from #BlackLivesMatter to #MeToo.

Slacktivism, where online activities are viewed as passive activism, is another facet. Like changing a profile picture to represent a cause, or sharing posts and signing online petitions, these seemingly insignificant actions can create waves of change.

Another novel form born out of social media activism is 'Doxing.' This practice involves publicizing private information about individuals, oftentimes with malicious intent, but has also been used as a form of protest or censure against perceived transgressions.

8.3. Social Media - A Platform for Empowerment and Protest

Social media empowers individuals by giving them an avenue to voice out their concerns, draw attention to issues, and mobilize collective action. Across the globe, people who have never met in person are uniting to effect change. The platforms allow users to share information quickly, organize events, raise funds for communal causes, and more. This user-centric approach has democratized activism, giving anybody with Internet access an equal opportunity to fight for causes they believe in.

However, social media has also been the venue for protest. Netizens have harnessed the power of these platforms to voice their discontent with how certain authorities or institutions manage or handle crises. The effectiveness of such protests largely depends on the strength of the message and its resonance with a broad audience.

8.4. The Role of Social Media in Community Organization

The capacity to unite communities in and outside of a geographical vicinity is one of social media's great wonders. Communities can unite for a collective purpose, be it addressing neighborhood problems or participating in broader society's movements.

One example of social media enhancing community organization is the neighbourhood social network application, Nextdoor. This platform connects neighbours together, disseminating information regarding local events, services, public safety alerts, and a venue for discussion about municipal matters.

8.5. Balancing Social Media Engagement, Activism and Mental Health

Despite the numerous benefits to be derived from social media activism, maintaining a healthy balance between our online engagements and mental health is critical. The inundation of issues, constant exposure to societal ills, alongside the impulse to act, can trigger heightened stress, anxiety, and emotional exhaustion, which can jeopardize mental wellbeing.

Setting boundaries, taking breaks from social media, diversifying our news sources, and finding tangible ways to channel our activism, such as volunteering for a cause or lobbying for policy changes, will help sustain our sanity and maintain the potency of our activism.

In conclusion, social media has gifted us an avenue to rally around issues that matter the most, opening doors to unprecedented forms of community engagement and activism. However, we must approach it with mindfulness and always strive to balance our mental wellbeing while engaging in online activism. Its potential is immense, and used judiciously, it can significantly shape the society of tomorrow.

Chapter 9. Bridging the Digital Divide: Ensuring Inclusive Community Resilience Efforts

The evolution of the digital age suggests a utopian vision where information is accessible to all, overcoming barriers of geography, socio-economic conditions, generations, or even disabilities. Yet, this often overshadows a key reality, a chasm popularly referred to as the 'Digital Divide', physically invisible but societally impactful: certain groups find themselves entrenched on the wrong side, unable to avail benefits of this expansive realm due to lack of accessibility, affordability, digital literacy, or even awareness.

9.1. The Anatomy of the Digital Divide

In the context of community resilience, the digital divide allows those privileged with access and knowledge to leapfrog ahead, leaving behind the underprivileged—even though some of the major challenges faced by societies need collective solutions that draw from diverse knowledge reservoirs. Complicating this divide are numerous dimensions: from geography, where urban residents have a clear advantage over rural folks; to the economic, where income levels dictate the ability to afford and access technology; to age, where digital natives (typically younger individuals) seem to be in a different world than digital immigrants (typically older individuals); to the disparities manifested along lines of race and gender. Understanding these facets of the digital divide is the first step towards devising strategies to bridge it.

The first dimension is geographical. Rural populations, especially in developing countries, often lack reliable internet access. Infrastructure constraints, from electricity to telecommunication towers, stymie attempts to bring them into the digital fold. The urban vs rural digital divide has significant implications for community resilience. In crises, real-time connectivity allows smoother logistics and quicker response times.

The economic dimension cannot be underestimated either. Not everyone can afford internet access, let alone own a digital device like a smartphone or a laptop. It's worth noting that often, lack of affordability isn't just about the inability to buy a device or pay for the internet—it's also about not being able to invest in learning how to use these resources.

The age divide is evidenced by the evident chasm between digital natives and digital immigrants. Irrespective of the availability or affordability of digital resources, digital immigrants are often not comfortable using these. There is a real and under-appreciated divide here which impacts how different age-ranges interact, engage and derive benefits from the digital world around them.

Then, there is the gender divide with significant gender disparities in access to and use of digital technologies. Women are less likely than men to have access to digital technology and the internet, particularly in lower-middle-income countries. They may also lack the confidence or knowledge to use digital tools effectively.

The racial divide further exacerbates the issue. Lack of investment in minority-dominated communities often results in them having poor digital infrastructure as compared to other communities, thereby severely impacting their ability to participate in the digital society.

9.2. Creating Inclusive Digital Solutions

In order to foster community resilience, it's important to work towards minimizing these divides. A multi-pronged approach involving policy intervention, infrastructural development, educational initiatives, specific inclusiveness programs targeted at demographic disparities, and awareness campaigns are some methods to promote inclusivity.

Policy initiatives should focus on making affordable digital access a basic human right. Governments could provide subsidies where required, support telecommunications companies to widen their reach, and enforce regulations to keep costs in check.

Educational initiatives will help build a digitally literate populace. Government and community-led training programs can play a pivotal role in nurturing digital proficiency amongst older generations, and within economically disadvantaged communities.

For marginalized communities, inclusive design needs to be promoted. Accessibility needs to be at the forefront when creating new digital platforms so that persons with disabilities, and those who are not technically proficient can also use such platforms effectively.

Awareness campaigns should focus on enlightening communities about the importance of getting digitally connected, the benefits of such connectivity, and how to practice digital safety. Such campaigns could manifest in various forms, from hands-on workshops led by digital natives to multimedia campaigns on traditional media outlets accessed by the digitally excluded.

Inclusive community resilience efforts are inextricably linked with appropriate digital literacy and access to all. A digitally inclusive society not only builds community resilience but also focuses on an equitable digital society where every individual can utilise the tools at their disposal to influence change, respond to crises, and thus, truly reap the benefits of the digital revolution.

In conclusion, stemming the tide of the digital divide cannot be the responsibility of a few. It requires concerted efforts from governments, businesses, educators, and even everyday netizens. As we place more value on connection, let's ensure we are connecting with everyone. Only then can we truly boast of a digitally inclusive community that embodies resilience, and where everyone, irrespective of age, location, or social background, can contribute to its betterment. The dream is a place free from exclusion—a place where each 'like', 'share', or 'tweet' can shine as a beacon of collective strength, equanimity, and resilience. We are marching towards that equitable future, one byte at a time.

Chapter 10. Guidelines for Leaders: Building Resilient Communities via Social Media

The ribbon unfurls to place leaders at the forefront of community resilience, elucidating their instrumental role in harnessing the power of social media. As we delve into an array of strategies beneficial for community leaders, it is essential to remember that each community is distinctive—hence, it is crucial to tailor these strategies according to the community's unique needs and characteristics.

10.1. Understanding the Basics: Resilience and Social Media

To build a resilient community through social media, leaders must first become well-acquainted with the concepts of resilience and the mechanisms of social media platforms. A resilient community essentially refers to a community that is capable of bouncing back effectively from adversities by utilizing internal resources and strength. In terms of social media, it is necessary to appreciate its ubiquity, multi-functionality, and penetration into various facets of modern life.

Social media platforms offer unique opportunities for leaders because they allow for immediate, two-way communication. Whether it is to inform, educate, or listen, these platforms provide an unfiltered channel between leaders and their communities. By leveraging these platforms effectively, leaders can foster an environment that promotes learning, mutual understanding, and resilience.

10.2. Building Trust and Credibility Through Authenticity

In the realm of social media, authenticity is the currency of trust. It is essential for leaders to create an authentic digital persona that reflects their real-world principles, morals, and leadership style. This can be achieved by sharing success stories, showcasing community work, and emphasizing the community's achievements. Leaders should also be open to receiving comments, suggestions, and criticisms because the very essence of resilience lies in adaptation and improvement.

Moreover, leaders should regularly engage with followers not only to disseminate information but also to build relationships. Leaders can show their personal side by sharing their hobbies, interests, and thoughts—this personal touch resonates with the audience and further elevates the level of trust.

10.3. Leveraging Social Media for Effective Crisis Communication

A resilient community is a well-prepared one, and social media can provide an immediate, expansive channel for crisis communication. Leaders can use platforms like Twitter, Facebook, and Instagram to provide real-time updates, correct misinformation, and counteract rumors during crises.

Accompanying messaging with images, infographics, or short videos can also increase the visibility—and thereby the impact—of the message. Social media can also facilitate the coordination of relief efforts by connecting respective stakeholders, including citizens, government agencies, non-profit organizations, and local businesses.

10.4. Promoting and Fostering Citizen Engagement

Active citizen participation is the backbone of a resilient community. Leaders should encourage their community to voice opinions, discuss pressing issues, share personal narratives, and contribute ideas. Engaging constituents on social media can take many forms—from simple Q&A sessions, polls, online debates, to creating groups or forums for community-specific matters.

Leaders can also turn these platforms into a pedestal to celebrate community members who exhibit resilience or contribute substantially to the resilience-building cause. Highlighting their effort on social media can foster a sense of belonging and create a culture of resilience in the community.

10.5. Training and Skill Development

Despite the widespread use of social media, not all community members may be well-versed in digital literacy. Leaders must ensure that their community has the skills to effectively use and comprehend online platforms. Conducting digital literacy workshops, offering online security tips, and guiding individuals on recognizing fake news are just some ways leaders can empower their community. By promoting digital literacy, leaders are helping to guard against fake news and cyberattacks—essential elements of digital resilience.

Another vital aspect is to adequately train community managers, digital communicators, and social media strategists. Equipping these individuals with the necessary knowledge and skills will ensure that social media campaigns are impactful, informative, and engaging.

10.6. The Ethical Consideration

Finally, leaders must always prioritize ethical guidelines when using social media. Transparency, respect for privacy, consideration of cultural diversity, and refraining from the spread of misinformation should form the foundation of any online interaction.

As we collectively navigate the intertwined physical and digital landscapes of community life, we find leaders standing firm on the pedagogy of resilience. With this guide, they have the tools they need to leverage social media to its full potential in taking their communities towards newfound resilience. This is not just about a group of people recovering from a disruption—it's about them thriving amidst it, their spirits unbroken, their resolves strengthened. Armed with hashtags and likes, retweets, and shares, leaders are set to build a network of resilient communities, with fibers running across the globe, bolstered in unity. Leadership, after all, is about influence. And in the digital age, what better way to influence than through the power of social media?

Chapter 11. Looking Ahead: The Future of Community Resilience in a Connected World

As we stand on the verge of a boldly connected world, the interplay between community resilience and the sprawling ecosystem of social media beckons a future ripe with limitless perspectives. This seamless unity offers the chance for communities to leap forward, benefitting immensely from the swift surges of technological progress and the boundless compass of human creativity. In this vein, exploring the future of community resilience within the context of a digitized globe is warranted, necessitating inclusivity, adaptability, innovation, and abundant collaboration.

11.1. Unveiling the Landscapes of the Future

Upcoming decades are likely to witness an increasingly interconnected socio-digital realm. As per several future outlooks, social media is projected to evolve beyond a mere communication platform, maturing into an integral facet of our lives transcending geographical boundaries and cultural divides. Consequently, this shifts its role in shaping community resilience from an instrumental facet to an indispensable thread intricately woven into the societal fabric. Harnessing this evolution bravely will demand communities to adapt to dynamic disruptions, adopt emerging technologies, and above all, stay deeply rooted in empathy and inclusivity.

Massive advancements in Artificial Intelligence (AI), Machine Learning (ML), Internet of Things (IoT), and other contemporary technologies hold immense promise for social media-driven community resilience. AI, along with predictive algorithms and big data analytics, can provide real-time insights into community needs, patterns, and potential threats, enabling swift mobilization and coordination of response efforts. IoT, on the other hand, could foster the integration of physical and digital spaces, thus providing numerous platforms for community engagement and resilience-building activities.

11.2. Navigating the Challenges Ahead

Whilst the convergence of community resilience and social media proposes immense potential, it also brings forth significant challenges. Instances of misinformation, digital illiteracy, privacy breaches, and the digital divide introduce the need for robust frameworks to safeguard community interests while leveraging social platforms for resilience.

Addressing misinformation is paramount in ensuring that only credible and valuable information circulates within the digital community. Introducing reliable fact-checking tools and developing stricter content regulation policies might be potential solutions. Education and awareness campaigns focusing on digital literacy, safe social media use, and privacy protection can mitigate the risk of cyber threats and empower individuals to navigate digital spaces confidently. Further, to bridge the prevailing digital divide, affordable and equitable access to technology and the internet needs to be realized as a global priority.

11.3. Shaping Resilient Communities: Embracing Technological Innovation

Leaders and authorities, while employing technology and social platforms, must ensure these tools ingrain community resilience in every fragment of the society. Developing open-source platforms promoting collaborative efforts within the community, harnessing blockchain technologies for transparency in operations, or developing AI-powered applications for disaster prediction and mitigation—there are multifaceted ways in which technology can boost community resilience.

Decentralized and encrypted platforms could enhance community trust and participation in shared resilience efforts, leading to a more engaged and resilient community. AI could aid in better vulnerability mapping, helping communities prepare and adapt for upcoming challenges efficiently. Virtual or augmented reality applications could revolutionize community education and preparation programs about disaster preparedness, facilitating immersive and effective learning experiences.

11.4. Co-creating a Resilient Future

Reflecting on the future of community resilience in a connected world, it is clear that the journey forward demands our collective energy, wisdom, and imagination. As social media continues to grow, diversify, and influence our lives, it becomes essential to harness this powerful tool consciously, creatively, and compassionately.

In this unfolding story of resilience and connection, everyone has a part to play. Governments, civil society, businesses, technical communities, and individual citizens have roles that intersect and align. Each can contribute to resilience-building efforts, shaping a future defined by shared strengths and mutual support.

Together, we are on the cusp of a new era. An era where resilience lives not just in the robustness of our infrastructures and systems, but in our collective agency and the strength of our digital connections. We can create the future we envision—one where community resilience thrives in the face of hurdles, one sustained by the unique, potent force of our interconnected world.

www.ingramcontent.com/pod-product-compliance
Lightning Source LLC
Chambersburg PA
CBHW071008260726

48661CB00007B/2847